D0953258

TO BE THE POET

The William E. Massey Sr.
Lectures in the History of
American Civilization

TO BE THE POET

Maxine Hong Kingston

HARVARD

UNIVERSITY

PRESS

CAMBRIDGE,

MASSACHUSETTS

LONDON,

ENGLAND

2002

DRAWINGS AND ENSOS ARE BY THE AUTHOR

Library of Congress Cataloging-in-Publication Data

To be the poet / Maxine Hong Kingston.

p. cm.—(The William E. Massey, Sr. lectures in the
     history of American civilization)

ISBN 0-674-00791-3 (alk. paper)

1. Kingston, Maxine Hong.

2. Authors, American—20th century—Biography.

3. Chinese American women—Biography.

4. Poetry—Authorship.   I. Title.   II. Series.

PS3561.I52.Z48 2002

813'.54—dc21

[B]   2002017261

To Earll, always

CONTENTS

TO BE THE POET

I CHOOSE
THE POET'S LIFE

chapter one

I have almost finished my longbook. Let my life as Poet begin. I want the life of the Poet. I have labored for over twelve years, one thousand pages of prose. Now, I want the easiness of poetry. The brevity of the poem. Poets are always happy. I want to be always happy. No plotting any more plots. For the longbook (about the long wars in Viet Nam and in the Middle East), I sacrificed time with my child, grown and gone, and my husband and family and friends, who should have been loved more. The longbook has got to be done soon, and I'll be free to live. I won't be a workhorse anymore; I'll be a skylark. Free of obligations. I am sixty years old; I have enough reputation and fame and money. Poets don't care too much for money. I declare to you: I'm making a try for poetry. Say one becomes Poet by grace . . . beauty and truth hap upon the Poet

. . . all gift, no labor . . . the Muse flies over, and drops jewels
upon the Poet's head and into open hands . . . I will go about
lifting an empty basket to the air.

I want poetry to be the way it used to come when I was a
child. The Muse flew; I flew. Let me return to that child being,
and rest from prose. My mother used to hold me by the waist,
and boosted me out the upstairs front window. "Sing to your
grandfathers," she said. "Tease them." My mother's hands at
my waist squeezed poems out of me.

> Som Goong ah.
> Say Goong ah.
> Nay hoy nai, yah?
> Mah hai cup cup,
>   say ngyeuk, yow say ngyeuk,
> Nay hoy nai, yah?

Here's the translation of my very minor Chinese dialect:

> Hey, Third Grandfather.
> Hey, Fourth Grandfather.
> Where are you going?

Horse shoes clippity-clopping
four feet, then four feet,
Where are you going?

My two grandfathers sat atop the stagecoach drawn by two black horses, and laughed, and clapped their hands. "Ah," they said. "Ah-h-h." Let me have poetry to be like that once again, and I shall die happy.

When I was in the fourth grade, Mrs. Garner taught us to make a copybook entitled *Gems*. *Gem* was another word for *poem*. She fitted five pieces of chalk into the fingers of the wood-and-wire thing, drew music lines on the blackboard, and copied gems. We copied them into our books, and we owned them. One day, I heard and felt a rush of wings. Down through the roof and in through the windows came golden light, and words streaming in couplets and quatrains and long, long stanzas. . . . *fly* . . . *I* . . . *sky* . . . *cry* . . . *die* . . . *why* . . . *fly* . . . *fly* . . . All the important words rhyme. They blow out of the sky, and all I have to do is write them down.

I want days as a Poet. Not the workaday life of the prose-writer. I am still on the longbook job. The workhorse day is never over. You can make yourself write prose into the evening, and on into the night. Rise before dawn to elude the people you live with. Think, think, think, plot, plot, write, write, write. Faithfully go at it. Apply yourself to a question, explain things, follow the characters wherever they go. Labor away, and there will be yield—the longbook.

The Poet's day will be moment upon moment of gladsomeness. Poets do whatever they like. They take off whenever they please—to the garden or the shops or the park for strolling or rollerblading. They dine with friends. They go dancing. They go to the library, and read a book that has nothing to do with research. They nap in the hammock, cook, have tea and cookies, invite people over, visit them, pick up the ringing telephone, play music, watch t.v., do nothing, do nothing but breathe. The Muse will find you, and hand over poems. The writing down will be short, and the day long, hardly any of it spent actually writing. The poem comes unworked for. You just pick up the gold fountain pen or the glass pen with the spiral nib, dip it in ink, touch the fine linen laid paper, and out flows the poem. Practicing, I am writing this lecture at my parents' roll-top desk, which they took from the gambling house. My father used to sit here with fountain pen and brush pen, writing, and my mother with pencil and ballpoint, first draft, later drafts. They both wrote letters and histories. Once in a while, he'd write down a poem, then a poem from memory, then another poem "that just came to me." My father did the calligraphy on cloth; my mother embroidered the poems. And they sang them a cappella.

I have more than a lifetime's supply of ink. My father made his own ink, and left a dozen liters in ridged and beveled bottles, corked like wine. It settles and separates into pretty layers, like pousse-café. Shaken, it turns blue or brown. I decanted some into an inkpot; the dip pen stood in it, ready. That ink is so strong, it ate away the nib.

I can will a longbook. The novel can be willed. But a poem is good luck. "Lucky," said my mother. The poet is lucky. I can't help it; I am willing poetry. I will poetry.

I take after my father, worrying over poetry. I inherit his ink; I inherit his questions. "What is a poem?" he'd ask. "Is this a poem?" "Why don't poems come to me constantly, the way they came in China?" My mother tried nagging him into poetry: "Where are the poems, Poet?" William Carlos Williams would answer: Poetry comes out from the ground, and from people. My father couldn't hear language in America as he could in China. "How can a poem ever be translated from one language to another?" Chinese and English—different tones, different tunes, different hemispheres of world and mind.

Why does the Muse of Lyric Love Poetry have a name that sounds like "Error"? Is it that she has wandering wings? What if she doesn't choose me? I'm still occupied with the long-book. She's waiting for me to be free. The Poet is free. Worriers and fretters do not attract poetry.

Ten years ago, I turned 50 at a party where a lot of men were also turning 50—Malcolm Margolin, Bob Hass, Richard Nelson, Lee Swenson. They gloated—the luckiest generation, born in the luckiest year, dragons all—children when there was still country, farm life, and wildlife, young men without the draft, didn't go to any of the wars, had sex during the sexual revolution—the pill—and they bought a house before real estate cost too much. And they were alive to hear such musicians, such Poets.

Gary Snyder, elder, responded, "Poets get away with a lot."

I asked what he meant. Poets leap? They skip scientific

proofs and mathematical steps? And alight wherever they please? Poets don't have to build bridges?

Gary Snyder, who is now writing much prose, including footnotes, said that critics don't criticize poets. "For some reason," he said, "the people who read poetry are shy to criticize it. Prosewriters get criticism and scrutiny. But readers of poetry are shy to criticize poets." *So*, poets are even free of critics!

Whenever I meet a poet, I ask: How will poetry come to me? What are the ways?

At a dinner party that Nick Delbanco gave for Raymond Carver and Tess Gallagher, with Jay McInerney and John Aldridge also there, I asked Tess how she gets poems. She said that the night before poetry-writing day, she reads poems. Poetry-writing day is a free day; she is quiet and alone. She lights candles, and "invites the poems." "I face the coming or not-coming of the poem with neither hope nor despair."

On the deck of a boat sailing the Li River between the mountains that look like the mountains in ink brush paintings, I was standing between William Gass and Allen Ginsberg. Allen made up a poem on the spot—an exact description of the people around us, and the sunrays that fanned from a mountain's cleft. (Well, not perfectly exact, calling peo-

ple "Japanese tourists" who were Cantonese tourists.) I asked
Bill Gass, "How do you feel, watching him do that when
you've been working on your longbook for twenty years?"

"It took him twenty years to learn spontaneous composi-
tion."

Allen Ginsberg instructs: "First thought, best thought." Oh,
to have my every spontaneous thought count as poetry! No
draft after draft like a draft horse.

Clayton Eshleman, laughing, said, "'First thought best
thought' is not 'First *word* best *word*.' Ginsberg does rewrite.
I'm sure he does."

I have noticed that prosewriters like the company of prose-
writers, and poets, poets. Barry Lopez looked over at *them*,
and said, "Amateurs. We're the pros. They're the amateurs."
Jim and Jeanne Houston's address is "The Prose Channel."

Writing and reading have to do with time, playing with
time, stretching it into eternity, pinning its moments down.
The reader of the longbook lives with the story and its charac-
ters for a long time. The reader of poetry is awakened to the
one moment. The Poet truly lives the happening moment,
and gives the very bodily feeling of it to whosoever would

read. To put myself into the state of poetry, I need to learn the habit of living constantly within the present moment.

I will be selfish. There's a wonderful moment I have on the verge of sleep—I have nothing to do but feel my feelings, look at the pictures behind my eyes, and go to sleep. Consider no one but myself. Rest from the social responsibility of prose. Don't care about people's antics anymore. I will be socially irresponsible. I will be a Poet.

I'm going to set up a place somewhere, an orderly, beautiful place, where I will be alone and happy and poetic. Phyllis Hoge, who lived in the Poet's Cottage downhill from my Big House, wears headphones to hear no noise but white sound. I would be wandering about in the old blue-ginger garden, and espy her. I evaded her, and she evaded me.

I asked Alice Fulton how she gets the poems to come. She says that she clears the coming day. No appointments on poetry day. She finds a comfortable place—she likes comfort; she called the dinner I cooked for her "comfort food"—and she stays in bed surrounded by things and books that she loves. Have fun, and the poems come. You have to give it all day. "I need the expanse of the day." Alice gets such a day but once a week. She tells students with poetry troubles to watch mute t.v. and invent the sounds, use their own words. "Students work so hard; they need permission to watch television. Play, and the poetry comes."

I'm teaching school this Spring semester, but the longbook is almost done. I should be able to make more than one day per week an empty day. I'll bring my fountain pens and nib pens and inkwells and a notebook of beautiful paper to the meditation room, sit on the tatami floor, and use the bamboo bench as a desk. I will start on the first day of Spring.

One of my god-daughters was told at the age of 12 that she will never be a prima ballerina. She's only good enough for the corps. I hate that. There shouldn't be disciplines—ballet, football—where you don't get a chance to existentially construct yourself, yes, even the physical body. Learn, work hard, and make your very body.

I was there in Ho Chi Minh City when Larry Heinemann said his poem to Vietnamese listeners. He told of beginning the day, standing in the back yard, drinking his morning coffee. Suddenly, rushes of winds—wings—fly close over his head, fan his skin, lift his hair. A pair of Canada geese arrow past him, and call him, call him. "Just tell it like it happened. Tell how it came, and you have your poem. A piece of cake."

I witnessed Fred Marchant in the act of making a poem. Poets of Hûé took us to the top of a pyramid in the middle of the night, and sang poems at a place on the stone that amplifies voices. Fred felt pressure to come up with poetry on the spot. (I, prosewriter, felt no such importunity.) He described the moment we were living—us looking at one another, the stars and the moon (full that night) looking at us, the headlights of our car (turned on so we could see to climb) looking too. "I think sometimes Hûé is the center of the universe, / that thousands of eyes have turned towards us here. / . . . The blinding eyes of the van's headlights. / And the soft pinpoints of candles cradled on the river. / The eyes of the many no longer here. / And the loving eyes of friends who are." At publication of "Hûé, in Darkness," Fred changed "loving eyes" to "living eyes." "And the living eyes of friends who are." Touring Hûé in the morning, I saw temples with an eye painted above the entrance, and a gigantic global eyeball next to the altar. The idea of eyes, seeing and being seen, must manifest itself powerfully here, and the poets and religious people feel it.

I *have* written what has passed for poetry. (My father would ask, "Are these poems?") Gary Gach invited me to contribute to *What Book!? Buddha Poems from Beat to Hiphop.* I was still working on the longbook, no time for poetry, so I gave him my diary-like notebook, a daybook, and he included me as a Zen Poet. Read these, and you decide: are they poems?

25 December
Write before other people get up. Dress.
Let the other people have at the day.
Stay conscious. Give them insurance
to ink. Afternoon—write when they leave.
Go to Carmen's house, see Joseph.
Evening before bed—write.

26 Dec.
An idea—that the process is
best when easy. "Calm. Ease."
Drive to Berkeley. Call John.
Dinner out—S.F.?—

And the way to control anything
is to be aware of it.

                              Thursday
        Today, woke up remembering
and looking ahead. Tried to
focus by meditation.
Then made alarm go
off in pool house—the
alarm had gone off
at *3:50* or so, and I
went out to fix it—
Earll turned on the news,
made him stop—
Postum and wrote (an
idea came during meditation)—now I'll
have breakfast, write,
make the bed, dress.
At 9:00 or so—make calls—
the architect, check list
of calls. Write some more.

Maybe shower at Bessie's.
Invite her to dinner at
Faculty Club? Is there
anything I need at her
house? The mail &
calls. <u>In the American</u>
<u>Grain</u>. School—go a
little early—apptmts.
Dinner. Work on
writing, letters,
insurance.
Saturday—Began w/ meditation.
Write. Decide whether to go to
the framers. Letters to Nikki
Giovanni, Mary Gordon,
Toni Morrison.

                              February 20, 1992

Very upset on verge of cold
& coffee. Today, concentrate
on one thing at a time—

you don't have to say or
do everything. Write—
then collect things for Bessie's
house. Check on plane
tickets. Have grapefruit.
Picture for Cal Book—
School. Go to *35 up*
movie? Get some black ink.

26 May

Today—plan the future—Phone
Jeannine to add another day.
Phone New York & change
the film date. Phone
Krueger to talk about the
plans. Go to school, shop
for the bed.
4:15 P.M. woke up from nap—earlier—bought
bed, called Krueger's & Joseph—
some writing—grades in.

~

This afternoon, do some writing,
clean the house. School
is over—nice talking w/
Larry to end it—3 months
before school starts.

Do some writing. Organize house.
    Maybe finish the insurance.

            ~

Forgot the mail. Forgot to
do banking

                        27 May

    Not bad meditation—
normal, sweet—water
plants—
Last night's dream—
ladders take us to
heaven & other side
of darkness & bottom
of planet—it will
be a long time before

my father & I will
be together again.
The ladders up to
Mom's house / bedroom
where if we put food
the birds come, &
the animals are
from Pop's world.
Mom says don't feed
them & let them in the house.

~

Suddenly free from the lie
that my parents had me
for the purpose of torturing
me.
    How did I become convinced
of such craziness?
    And how did I get free?

~

Thought about *3:15* A.M. Oct. 27, 1992
    written afternoon next day—

in the Japanese room.

The street corner orderly
the lines, trees as is—
just right.

The dawn took forever
until I learned it
was the middle of the night

and I was wide-awake
jet-lagged

Dark with streetlights—
still—no traffic and
no people

Respite—the exact
present moment

The way the light falls
    is perfect

A reader of *What Book!?* asked me to sign the part about my parents not having me in order to torture me. She said,

"Those words are very important to me." To her, those lines
are certainly poetic. But I think Gary Gach published my
pieces because of the significant dates, Christmas, my birth-
day, and the names of famous people. Too much left out
that needs explaining. The insurance was for the fire in
the Berkeley/Oakland hills that burned 3500 houses, our
house, and my longbook, and killed 25 people. We lived
with friends, and took showers at this one and that one's
house. Poems shouldn't rely on missing information for
mystery.

In early February, to find a poem, I accepted my brother
and sister-in-law's invitation to see the elephant seals at Año
Nuevo. Taking the day off, I was already acting like the Poet.
The prose writer of the longbook never goes on spontaneous
outings. After waiting for two hours, we were given places in a
tour group and hiked toward the ocean. I saw my first ele-
phant seal hiding behind a sand dune, alone and taking a nap,
perfectly still. I thought she was dead. She looked like a dead
cigar. Her nostrils were shut and she was not breathing. She
can live underwater. Over and around the range of sand, we
saw between us and the ocean, a valley, a field of elephant
seals. Harems of elephant seals. Males were rearing up, fight-

ing, roaring, slamming chest to chest and biting necks. Each
fighting pair were giant black red-wounded hands thrust up
out of the earth, clasping and clenching. The males have a
snout like a finger or a wattle or a penis that flops on their
face. They are not attractive; the females try to get away from
them. A huge elephant seal came up out of the sea. The ex-
panses of blubbery skin on the beach rippled, and moved in-
land. A female would see him galumphing forth, scream, and
try to bury herself in the middle of the harem. Without legs,
the seals squirm on the ground; they hop and pull themselves
along with their front flippers. The big male fresh out of the
sea caught a female, and plopped on her. She screamed and
screamed. Ow. Ow. The other females, relieved that it wasn't
them getting fucked, stopped trying to escape, relaxed. A fe-
male lost from her harem will get jumped and injured by too
many males. The loser males go off alone; some jump the
pups. The females are a third or a fourth the size of the males.
It would be hell to be reincarnated as a female elephant seal.
The estrus smell leaks out, and targets you for rape, running
with no legs. A baby pup, lost from its mother, tries to nurse
on a loser male, who bites it. A seagull stands on a lost,
shrunken, skinny pup and pecks on it. Babies huddle together

so they look like one bulky seal. You can see the belly buttons of those on their backs. Mothers are calling for their lost baby, and there are babies crying for their mother; none of them find each other. The park rangers do not try to match them up; they let the lost pups starve to death. The rangers did interfere with nature when they removed a plastic ring from around a seal's neck. We could see the scar where the ring had cut into him. Sometimes a compassionate "inexperienced" mother will let as many as four lost pups nurse on her; none of the babies gets enough milk, she weakens, and they all die. A mother opens her mouth wide and bites the lost weaner on his back where the tail starts. Masses of seals fucking and biting and sleeping in mud and orange shit. They do not loll; they don't like the sun. I want to wade into their midst, and sort everything out. (Quick, before it knows what hit it, put the starving pup out of its misery.) Let's have some rules around here. Where is your code of ethics?

The park ranger led us up a path between dunes to see another group of seals. The people ahead of me turned around, running in a panic; I turned and ran too. A 5,000-pound bull seal was chasing us. We were in his path. *He* was being chased by another bull seal, and *he* was being chased by *another* bull elephant seal, the alpha male. A rampage of sexed-up seals—an alpha male, a beta male, and a C-minus male, chasing the human beings.

One merciful rule that Nature does have: Seals don't eat in this mess. They eat at sea when all the mating and weaning are over. They give birth at sea too. At sea, they're clean and free. They don't need anything, not even air. They'll move, swim, fly far distances. Most of the year, they are on a wonderful ocean voyage.

Of all my observations about the elephant seals at Año Nuevo, this last bit about flying through the ocean is the only part that seems poem-like to me. I wish I could see them free and eating, and know their lives to be happy.

It is 17 days until Spring. All will change. On the vernal equinox, I vow, I shall fly from prose to poetry. I hear Mike Wong's voice say, "Patience." I hear Britt Pyland say, "I wish for patience." My enlightened friends counsel patience. I think they mean: to live slowly, not to be skipping ahead to the next thing. It's my bad habit to get whatever task over with so I can live.

After my longbook burned in the fire, I gathered war veterans to have people to write-in-community with. We're mostly prosewriters except for Ted Sexauer. He gave us instruction for finding the way to poetry, to make the poems, to make the poems come. He entitles the method "How to feel—Exercise for integrating the internal with the external." A symptom of Post-Traumatic Stress Disorder is going numb; being well is to be able to feel. "Feelings make you human. Feelings make the writing alive." The Poet has feeling, and gives the reader feeling.

1. First pay attention to what you feel. (It may be one or more general feelings, or one in particular that is asking for attention.) Write one word or a phrase.

2. Close your eyes. Now what do you feel? Write it down.

3. Now look around yourself. What do you see? Write down one thing or several. Make them brief; do not use a complete sentence. (Unless you feel like it.)

4. Close your eyes again. How do you feel now? Write it down. Do not justify it; only acknowledge it.

5. Open your eyes. Write down what you see. Do not attempt to understand or process this. Do not question why.

6. Repeat this process until you are ready to stop.

7. Now find your personal way to put these words together.

Tonight please try feeling, seeing, noting, noting seeing, noting feeling. Let's try for poems. Let's meet tomorrow with poems in hand. May poetry come to one and all this night.

I CALL ON THE MUSES OF POETRY, AND HERE'S WHAT I GET

chapter two

On the First Day of Spring, I go to a writing retreat with war veterans at a farmhouse in the country. It is noon in Sebastopol. Facing west, I see hills and valleys. Straight over there would be the Pacific Ocean, and later the sunset. I open my eyes, write, close my eyes, write.

> The greengold leaves of the birch at the window
> shoot shadows of arrowheads onto the kitchen walls
>   and stove,
> and upon the bowed heads of war veterans.
> My skin and my heart awake and shiver
>   in corresponding delight.

I am not satisfied with this jotting as a poem. I have the prosewriter's desire for more story. For more.

The seventh and last step of the exercise-to-access-poetry is: "Now find your personal way to put these words together." It's this last step that would turn the notes into a poem. You gather your close-eyed experiences and your open-eyed experiences as raw words, then arrange them, add to them, exchange them for just-right words, and somehow make coherence. You are transmuted from note-taker to Poet.

I go outside, sit on the boards of the porch that overlooks valleys and hills, close my eyes, and hear the sounds of the first day of Spring.

> Roaring ~ Something rough and
> heavy is being dragged on asphalt ~
> It's the cold wind. My inside is soft and warm ~
> Today and usually, I am distinct from the world.

But that's not true. There is no strict divide between the world and me. Shutting the eyes does not shut out the environment, and my surroundings do not replace my emotions. What I feel influences what I see, and, of course, what I see affects my feelings. (What *is* feeling? Mere bodily sensation? Something at the edges of thought, but sometimes central.)

Doing the exercise-to-become-a-Poet, I was already living

the Poet's life. I came to rest. I took the time to be still, to be with friends, to behold them, to observe where I am, to have feelings, whatever the feelings might be. As a prosewriter of the longbook, I go off into the past, the future, the imagined world. The Poet alights in the right-now time, and stays in the special/ordinary moment. If I were to make an hour for poetry every day, I would change my life.

Now I am at home by myself, sitting on the tatami floor of the meditation room. My pens, pencils, and notebook are ready on the bamboo bench. My father's calligraphy hangs above me. "All World Human Peace." "Heart Spacious Spirit Happy." (In Chinese, these are complete sentences.) His was not the grass style but precise and legible. I will do the poetry exercise again, with more precision. I will very deliberately set down what's inside and outside.

Step 1 Inside: The stomach hurts. I am remembering dinner at a gourmet hamburger place last night. My stomach is hurting from the hamburger and the impatient waiter. He pushed the drinks and the side dishes. "Which salad do you want?" "Does a salad come with the hamburger?" "No." "Then I don't want it." "Shall I bring a bottle of water for the whole table, or do you want tap?" "Tap please." "Tap." "Me too. Tap." Earll knocked over his wine glass, red wine all over the white tablecloth. I'd ordered a burgundy, but got white wine. Chablis from Burgundy, stupid. The dinner conversation, the parts that most engaged me, was worries and brags about our children. I could write short stories or a novel-of-generations about us, our lifelong friends, and our children. I lead a prose life.

Step 2 Outside: The loving sun over the hills and onto gold straw and bamboo ~ I feel the sun loving my cheeks and hands.

Step 3 Inside: Continuous feel of sun, sounds of wind and cars pull me into my time here. I tug toward worries and errands, chores, t.v.

Step 4 Outside: I check the time: 8:44 A.M. I have been at this for half an hour. Sit on the bamboo bench/table and see the hills in the south ~

blue hills against blue sky,
the green cemetery and our houses,
my street trees (hackberries) that I tied plastic
bags around to signal the dog owners.
The bags hang low, blow and crackle,

dog eye and dog nose level;
the dogs will understand.
My five raised beds are full—lettuce, grown and bolting,
a lettuce tree, broccoli, snow peas. Can't see
the ruby red chard from here.

I am writing in lines! I get an instinct where to break, and jump—space. Could you hear that there are lines? Somehow different from sentences in a paragraph?

This next part comes in lines too:

Step 5 Inside:

Heart beating too hard again.
Bird uplilts, questions, questions. Asking what?

Step 6 Outside:

White family going into house where I
thought Black family lived.
Man with corgi—he has his own plastic bag—
stops and waits for his dog.
Oh, it's Kathy—she's turned about and
the plastic bag is weighted and swinging.

Good Kathy. Good Lucky.

Inside:

> The inside is speedy, impatient, stomach—unhappy
>   to my stomach—
> I vow to listen to music every night. You hear my vow,
>   I have to keep it.

Peeking outside: Spider web. Impatient for words, I'll draw the spider web.

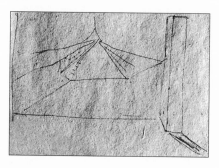

Inside: Worry: Whalen, Ferlinghetti, Ginsberg selling their notebooks for millions of dollars. I, prosateur, am giving away my papers, scratch paper, for free. Theirs are sheaves of hand-written poems, calligraphy, artwork.

You must hear that these last sentences were not in lines. Worries, ignoble thoughts, and petty feelings do not poetry make.

Outside: This paper is bejeweled with colors. I'd thought it was gray. My father left me clear calligraphy. It is after 9 A.M. now.

I know that the last step is to integrate and make better the words and the ideas. But I don't feel like rewriting just yet. At the end of a draft, the prosewriter can immediately go back to redoing the beginning. Enough time passes to see afresh. I went outside and picked all the winter broccoli, and arranged the enormous curving lobed blue leaves in the cut-glass punchbowl.

I read the directions for poetry again. I'd misconstrued Step 1, which says to pay attention to feelings. It does not say Open eyes, nor Close eyes. I assumed that I had to close my eyes to see my feelings. Try feeling with eyes open.

1. I feel: at rest but with worry tinges around the edges.

2. Eyes closed, I feel large Self and large warm World. I don't want this life to end.

3. I see my foot on tatami straw, and my hand on this paper. I touch and feel my wrinkles, veins, nails.

4. Closed eyes, I feel: an itch on my arm, which would be invisible to the eye anyway. Concern for Earll downstairs. For Joseph in Hawai'i.

5. I see: tops of houses, roofs, chimneys, tops of old trees, and my new brass bowl bell crooked on its stand.

6. I feel/think: Someday I'll return to these notes, and maybe they will form a poem. I'll entitle my collection "Spring Harvest." I feel tears well up. Unlike me to cry.

I feel tears upwelling, and falling.
One of those grotesque serial killers is getting his injection.
Right now. Near here. Outside San Quentin, Indians
    from three tribes (none his)
are drumming for him. Maybe he hears the drums.
Maybe his heart is affected.
Maybe he feels tears.
He'd been denied a sweat lodge—hot rocks dangerous—

I have to take out that line about a sweat lodge. It's a flash-back, and there's a passive-voice verb, and it doesn't have a word that rhymes with "tears." Internal rhyme pulled that event to mind. Can't give him a sweat lodge, give him a poem. Would it be too corny to write "may" instead of "maybe"?

> May he hear drums.
> May the drumming reach his heart.
> May he feel tears.

Strange, I hardly cry anymore except for political events, such as genocides, executions, wars.

March 21, 2000. The first day of spring:

1. Open-eyed feeling: Cough, hearing cars. If I were a car, I'm in neutral—an o.k. place to be. Appreciate the non-pain. Some anxiety, always.

2. Close-eyed feeling: Surprise. The large, living broccoli leaves flashed energy at me when I cut them.

3. I see—limit and focus to see—the bamboo bench, brass
   lantern and brass bell/bowl, and paper lamp that Lilah
   made.

4. Close-eyed, I feel the little beginning flowers of the
   broccoli as flames.

5. I see my glasses on the table. I am writing with glasses
   off. The broccoli flowers are yellow eyes. I feel the heat,
   they look at me.

I have a miracle—not a metaphor but a miracle. I actually felt
diamonds of light touch me.

~   ~   ~

Try for poetry day and night.
Try in various places.

~   ~   ~

Midmorning, the white daytime moon already waning,
    I stand on the south balcony. To my right, west,

Tamalpais clears the fog, blue hills, blue Bay, blue sky.
Birds are asking questions—no answers.
The mating cry is a question. Love me? Love me?
I tense, cold, go indoors, and look some more
    at Mt. Tam through the glass doors.
I'll come back here tonight to see what changes.
Evening—
    Large stars to the south
        —Mt. Tam gone.
    You know only from the ring
        of lights where the Bay ends.
    Blue-black cool air, land, water,
    the roar, traffic, ocean, pulse. Stay.
    Prolong the moment, and the day, and my life.
    It's because of the poetry plan that I have this time,
    and the place, the ground, the world also mine.
    My own dear Earth.
Night.
    I can't sleep tonight.
    William Stafford helps. "Freedom," the last stanza:

> If you are oppressed, wake up about
> four in the morning: most places,
> you can usually be free some of the time
> if you wake up before other people.

Awake in the middle of the night, I need only care for myself. Nothing happens. I don't have to do a thing. Nothing to do but watch the struggle/the interplay between being conscious and going unconscious. I won't mind dying. I will have relief from consciousness.

Image: Black wedges that will not flow,
     will not resolve into moving pictures.

Now I am sitting in the deacon's chair.

  I am under the skylight/the moon roof, a few stars.

  The hill houses are like stage sets;

  myriad unseen people are sleeping.

  A car on the hill-street rounds a curve.

  My brother drew the deacon's chair, and built it.

  Our walls are hung with baby holders and tapa.

  The bedroom door opens a crack—

    I peeked and saw Mother squatting over a basin of
      blood.

A baby cried, and through the top windowpane flew
a Christmas card like a bird, and announced my
   brother.
The sound of Earll in the water;
the shower is like rain in drought.
   Everything reminds me of everything.
I am almost old. Each thing
has a life of associations.

March 22, the Third Day of Spring 2000.
   Early morning, a bird is saying
   Me Me Me
   Do do do do

Birds

I'm living in one place so long,
the birds enlace their nests
with my white hair.

I'd like their recognizing me in return.
I play a game with hummingbirds.
I play the hose in jets and spouts,
and the hummer follows the water,

loops and soars, turns and hovers, leaps.
I shorten the arc toward myself,
and the hummer comes to my hands.
It enters the fine spray; it flies in the spray.
It alights on the tomato cage, and waits,
raises a wing, gets a squirt in one armpit,
and the other armpit. It shows its butt
and wiggles its tail. What's that gold thread?
The hummer is spraying me back.

There's a yellow bird that is barely anything
but a reed, a tube of song.
Its beak opens as wide as its throat, its body,
which trembles through and through.
It's a yellow-feathered skinbag of song,
and it sings all day.

The next day dawns.
I am at: the exact Real, and I myself am real,
bare feet and hands, feet on the floor,
hands writing, one holding the pen cap, the other
the pen. Walking and writing,

I look at, then away from the sun, higher and higher
warmth on my face.
A strand of web moves, runs, shines like an EEG line.
Palm fronds blow.
Windy day—all the natural things are blowing.
The man-made things are still but
for cars going their own ways.
Their grilles are solid smiles.
At the exact Real, myself real/true,
I am a smiling being.

a 3-line smile:

At my parents' rolltop desk (mine now)—neater than it's
ever been in their lives. 2 drawers empty—all the pigeonholes
nice and neat. Each of us kids had for ourself a pigeonhole or
a drawer or a space. In the knee well, a box of toys that be-
longed to all. This desk housed 8. I ringed a haku lei around
the shade of the pink lamp, which used to sit on their
nightstand. The photos are of my beloved people when they

were young. Woodblock prints from Hanoi—6 for a few dollars—Vietnamese have Monkey too. The clock ticks and ticks and ticks . . . Cold. Hungry. Go out in the sun amongst the Santa Barbara daisies. I'm trying not to roll on my rolling chair down the slope of this floor.

Stop to appreciate actions, business done:

> Made the phone calls.

> The check did come in the mail.

I know how to turn anything into worry on a to-do list. Fret. Fret. Fret. Fret.

At the hump of my back—the burden hump—the *chi* is stuck—like swallowing egg too fast.

The Chinese made list poems.

Enjoy my new Hanuman and Shiva lunch box. Hanuman Monkey wears a bell on his tail. Stay awake. Hanuman was a military general. I have misplaced two mindfulness bells, just when I'm learning not to lose glasses and keys so often.

On the bulletin board beside our desk:

> —The little boy jumps into the waves with open arms.

> —The sandhill crane jumps with wings lifted.

> All the cranes, and the boy, are facing west.

—Joseph and guitar with audience member. For
my son:

> joy in art
> good times
> music ~ beautiful timing
> people who love to hear him

Two yellow and black butterflies are dancing up and up to-
ward the sun.

I go outdoors, and I go indoors, hew chunks of time-for-
poems. Under the ticking clock. The White Rabbit is looking
at the clock. Beside the telephone. I have to phone. I have to
FAX bio-biblio info.

On the wall: My mother embroidered my father's callig-
raphy:

> Beyond mountains, yet mountains.
> Across seas, yet seas.

~   ~   ~

Now the bird is saying Come here. Come here.

The pocket knife I gave my father, and the pen—returned to me.

They—my mother and father—sat at this desk for fifty years each. The way they sat—they had been entirely here. They sat square in this chair. They concentrated. They wrote carefully, lovingly forming each stroke of each word. They re-wrote for the beauty of the handwriting. They did not need to clear a space; they wrote at the edge of the fish tank. Order was within them, and emanated from them.

Only write what I care to.

March 23—In my office at school
    I am out on my 4th-floor balcony.
    If it were not for poetry,
    I wouldn't've unjammed the doors,
    and be standing amongst the rooftops.
    Green hills surround me and the green
    copper eaves. A green copper pineapple
    caps the Library—Welcome. Welcome.
    Down through an immense copper-framed skylight,
    I can see a bookroom where I've never been.

The Campanile bongs and echoes into my nook.
I have been here a long time. Since I was young.
And the nearest buildings and the biggest trees,
the oldest trees also here long ago.
In the hills, away from trees, are the recent blocking
  cement structures—probably labs.
Sounds of planes and air conditioning.
Breezes touch me.
Clanging of dropped sewerpipes.
I should feel nostalgia for times gone but
I have this vista. This vista is my own.
  This place mine for staying till old.

March 24 Friday
  I will try three days with the attitude that I can control
    (my sense of) Time.
  I'll read the morning paper in the morning, despite
    bad news.
  I'll volunteer to cook lunch.
  I'll wait and watch the water heat up instead of going off
    to do something else.

I'll spontaneously return phone calls without premeditation for days.

I'll try not looking forward to the next meal, the next course.

"As soon as I get this over with, I'll start to live."

March 25 Saturday—I hardly tried poetry yesterday—knocked out by the longbook, which refuses to end. Months ago, two mornings, I awoke feeling: The longbook is over. But it keeps coming to me, and I keep writing it. "Over the river, more rivers / Over the mountain, more mountains." But my father had been happy singing that poem, and my mother illustrated it with birds in the trees and flowers, and birds in the water, and a dragon and a phoenix in the sky. Joy, and more joy. My father explained, "Learn, and learn more. Always more to learn." Infinities of wonders to learn. He did not mean trudging and drudging across continents.

March 26   The Poet's day:

Wander through the day, choose (among treasured

things), and wrap a gift, and give it away.
Sit and jot.
Wash the dishes after every meal and snack.
Run errands and know you are running errands.
Buy cheap beautiful notebooks.
Sit and jot some more.
Use each fountain pen.
Do not be so afraid.

March 27   I am 59 years and 5 months old, on an airplane.
I can write prose on plane rides, and in the car as Earll
drives. Engines—inertia takes over the body—do not allow
me tides. (Feelings come and feelings go, leave and return like
the tide. And the words are like tide lines.) The flow and wash
have stopped. I need to arrive and settle in. Gary Snyder's ad-
vice: Stay put. Yes, the happy life is one in which I get to stay
home.

April 1 at night at O'Hare airport—No poetic moment all
week on the move and in Ann Arbor. On to Europe. Hawai'i.
The Muse does not race airplanes. Carry this notebook con-

stantly, hold it to my chest. Looking forward to a large seat in first class, and sleep. I am grateful for my privileges. No words, I sketch some people around me: a vivid family from the Middle East, big dark eyes, scarves, hair, jewelry.

After dinner. These first-class seats recline almost all the way back. Dim light, boxed in by big arms, I feel safe and far from the daily cares, far from my duties. My habit: I think about going to die. Awful picture in paper today—African child sitting beside his starving curled-up father. The worst nightmare when raising our child: he would be afraid, alone beside my killed body. I used to worry, when my plane seemed to be going to crash, for my mother—how bad she'd feel. Godiva chocolates, port, cheese, and goodnight. The woman in the next seat, all in pink, pink clothes, pink nail polish, pink quartz, deals farm equipment world-wide, smiles with her whole soft pink face, says, "Good night."

Dinner with Alice Fulton and Hank De Leo. I asked again for secrets of poetry. She told me again that she makes a comfortable place for herself. "I surround myself with pleasures. Books. Notebooks." Hank said, "Alice is most ecstatic in the world of poetry, and also the most miserable." What can there be that is miserable in the world of poetry? "The low misery comes from the poeticians." Oh, but such a small art. Can't the Poet go about like fog on little cat's feet, and elude the marketeers and canoneers? "You have to work through the screen, through the wall the poeticians block you with. A poet saying you're shit." I wanted to, but didn't, descend into gossip, and ask Who. Come on. What Poet would call another Poet shit?

Poet should answer Poet with verse. Respond to the Poet with new poems.

William Carlos Williams's law of poetry: The American Poet must stay put on the ground of the Americas, and hear and be her voice.

In London, and whatever foreign place, I get that not-home feeling, as if I were dissipating. The cells and atoms of my body seem to be drawing apart. There is more space than matter. Strange smelling air blows against my forehead. At the Victory Services Club, we are greeted by a man without a hand. And here's a bent-over man. World I vet? The younger people could be from the Falklands War. Here's the placard on the door of our room:

> In memory of Brigadier J. Scott-Cockburn DSO NC
> Formerly of the 19th Royal Hussars and
> 4th/8th Queen's Own Irish Hussars

There are rooms and wings donated by Maharajahs and Malayan Rubber Growers' armies. Pictures of tanks and aerial dogfights line both sides of hallways. Planes and tanks in The Buttery cafeteria too. Not one memento of Viet Nam. The British were not in Viet Nam? I have negative capability—Keats's law of poetry—and know what's not there. No Viet Nam.

Earll spoke with the man with one hand, and told me that he did so have two hands. I take a good look—very long sleeves, two hands. (Earll plays John Wesley Powell on stage; a minie ball shot off an arm.)

We took a walk and had tea in Hyde Park. The speakers are from all over the world, and use their old languages; each has his share of audience. Our tea table is beside a lake. Two birds dancing atop the water. I've never seen such birds—long necks, long legs, long bills—facing each other and dancing.

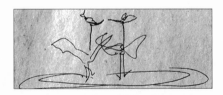

They look like flowers on long stems, stepping and flapping around and around, face-to-face do-si-do.

Calculating the last draft of the longbook—

$$
\begin{array}{r}
\phantom{10\,\text{pp/day)}}\underline{123\ \text{days to go}} \\
10\,\text{pp/day}\overline{)\,12\,30\ \text{pp rewriting}} \\
\underline{\phantom{10\,\text{pp/day)}}4\ \ 23/26\ \text{months to go}} \\
26\,\text{days/mo.}\overline{)\ 123} \\
\underline{10\,4} \\
\underline{23} \\
26
\end{array}
$$

But what's the difference, really, to the world and to my life, whether I finish the book within the month or the year, at 59 years of age or 60, in one millennium or another? As long as it gets written.

April 3—

Awake insomniac first night in London. Noises, traffic, tocsins. I picture red buses, square black cabs, emergency vehicles running all night.

We have breakfast in The Buttery. Watercolors of tanks. Watercolors of dogfights. Gurkhas in tans and sharp reds. At the next table, an Asian Caucasian family, mother, father, daughter and son, enjoying the food and one another's company. I myself must look like Earll's Japanese or Korean war bride.

Our war was Viet Nam. Earll and I talked about the veterans we know, their delicacy, their courtesy.

Afternoon jet-lag nap, I dreamed about veterans. One's face looked like this:

I've drawn a sphere, an orb with a dark opening in it. The opening is shaped like the island of Māui, like a two-ball snowman, like a dumb-bell gourd. The veteran was wearing a Hawaiian warrior's helmet, with a hole for mouth and eyes. Johnny Got His Gun's head. Hollows where eyes, nose, and mouth used to be. In dream, I see his eyes and recognize him.

Tonight, I set myself up in the library of the Victory Services Club. I'm sitting with my notebook and pen, and a glass of wine, in a wing chair by the window. Shoes off, feet up under my skirt. It's raining, and the black iron railings splash silver. The library belongs to old ladies. Once in the British military? The women vets are saying:

". . . Natural History Museum . . ."

". . . transport . . ."

"Brussels?"

". . . back of the bus . . ."

". . . Piccadilly Circus—buses go around the circus, around and around . . ."

Maybe they think I was a WAC, curled up and dozing at my Vets Club, aging, Asian, dreaming about war and peace, poeticizing.

April 4—an American chain café in London. I didn't want any more powdered decaf (Sanka) in The Buttery. Earll asks for "cream," and the server reaches under the counter and hands him a gallon of whipping cream. All the servers have coughs. An American customer yells, "I've been waiting for five minutes." He shouts his order, but turns and leaves, a red hot tail whizzing behind him. The servers look at one another and laugh, and cough. Screaming, irritating music should not be played this early in the day. Three Japanese girls with long disheveled frizzy hair enter; they should have left it long and straight. I look at myself in the mirror, and think, "She was a beauty in her day," which isn't true. I look better now, and so expect to continually improve.

~   ~   ~

Is there a law of poetry that lyric poems come to the young? And it's too late for me?

I'm watching t.v. B.B.C. T.V.
ought to be good for me.
Fellow watchers, veterans, Brits, men,
speak in numbers—22, 31, 42, 33.
They're comparing screen sizes.
They're not rating me.

Would the above six lines gain more interest if I were to entitle them "Foreigners"? For a story, I'd tell what we were watching, and the narrator would hang around long enough to interact with those men, and know their characters. Watching t.v. doesn't have much of a payoff. Grace Paley says, "By the third line, I know whether it's going to turn into a poem or a story. With poems, I talk to people. In stories, they talk to me."

~   ~   ~

Lolly Susi took us to her club, the Two Brydges. From the front of the Coliseum, we followed her down an alley, and went inside a tiny door, and up narrow stairs. Servants hung up our coats and brollies, and served us a lovely mid-day meal before the open fire. Lolly's an actress, an American, who got invited to join the club when she became a playwright. Now she awakes each morning looking forward to staying home all day writing her play. "I tell people I have appointments, but don't really. Life is fun."

~   ~   ~

April 5 Wednesday
    Train to Glasgow
    Pass rowhouses, a forsythia,
    a white-flowering tree,
    an estate on a green hill,

green hills and forests,
villages.
I am snuggled in my window seat.
A cell phone rings but not for me.
Snow in the far hills,
sheep in the meadows
brown and white horses
cattle and power stations
4 lambs sitting altogether
a church spire

Each thing runs into and joins the next thing,
and flits from graspy memory.
I'll draw the face of that African man, asleep.

Dots for his hair, an upside-down
    question mark for his nose.
He looks like my brothers.
The profile is supposed to be the
    hardest angle to draw,
        but maybe that's Caucasian faces.

Snow lumps beside the
    tracks
a lake
white trees in flower
stream past
Earll and the Black man
    fast asleep.

The Black man has on headphones. Music? A reading?
    Silence?
Earll's hand is over his heart.

~   ~   ~

I've forgotten all about training the inner eye upon the goings
on inside of me.
    La nausée. Slight, manageable wooziness from the train
        motion,
    and perfumes off a woman and a man pushing through,
    and the second-hand smoke I'm breathing.

Second-hand smoke poured into the car at the stops,
    out of the pubs and smokers on the platforms,
    and got trapped in here.
Concern for the neglected longbook.
Stagefright.
Places in motion.
Time in motion, wavering backward and forward.
Ear pressure—a tunnel.
Back to the world that enters through the eyes—
    houseboats along a river
    a church with graveyard
    vegetable gardens
    factories
    the town of Leighton Buzzard
On and on

        The on-and-on changes.

Change to the local to Stranraer at the end of the line.
Earll talks to an old railroad man, asks for connections
    to hear his Scotsman's voice tell about trains.

I draw him when he's not looking.

At Dumfries, there's a purple
station, trimmed in white.
 You can smell cattle through
shut doors and shut windows.
Tall clouds with flat bottoms
 skid aside,
  and reveal Sun.
 "Beautiful day." "Aye, beautiful day."
 "Nice day."
 "Lovely day, an't it?" "Yes, lovely."
We are saying, I feel good. I am happy.
 And, *You* are beautiful. *You* are lovely.

What I mostly think about while traveling—
 that we'll miss the train,

that we'll miss a connection,
that our reservations will have been lost,
and once on the right train,
that I'll have to ride backward.
I think about my students, who are on spring break.
This generation doesn't go for bacchanalian flings.
They're in Central America and Mexico and the
Philippines,
and seeing what they can do to help.
Another year, they'll return with skills and financing.
I send ribbons of white light, and rose light, and bands of
yellow,
on the out-breath toward the Americas and the Pacific,
and encircle everybody, and embrace them safe.

~   ~   ~

We have traveled a long way to see the friend
who has returned home
wounded from America.

We sit into the night, dark but for hearthfire.

The children go to bed; the dogs fall asleep.

We become hobgoblins—older faces,

    older shoulders, and old voices—

    and tell life stories of how we came to be here.

Her mother—she will look like her mother

    by the time her mother goes—

    speaks about the generations in this house.

Grandfather and great-grandfather worked the smithy in
back.

    The railroad ended that work.

Our friend, the daughter, tells about the theater

    where she's working. It used to be a farmhouse,

    then an inn, now a theater.

    A prompter sits in the middle of the front row and
      prompts.

    "Prompted me when I took a breath."

    We are that far away from Broadway and London.

Earll says that he loves the life on stage because

    you always know what will happen next and what to
      say next.

I say little. I ask for more. I'll be audience.

Saturday April 8   Swansea, where Dylan Thomas was born
        on October 27th, the same date I was born.
    I've never seen tide go out so far.
    "The furthest tide in the world."
    They're surfers in Swansea. Where's the surf?
    Large whole shells bestrew the endless wet land.
    So many species of cockles, mussles, clams,
        golden clams, and snails, and oysters,
        jewels I could follow away—until the tide
        turns and runs me over.
    I cannot see to the end of it, not a lip of sea.
    My life goes out. It goes out. It goes out.
    I shouldn't have tanned for 17 years in Hawai'i,
        which left lines and brown spots on my face.
        (The blue a tattoo—I jabbed my temple with a pen.)
    Old people fade. The black is gone from my hair,
        and leaving my eyes. My angles lose definition.
    I will stay put. The tide will come in and in and in.

April 10   Home
    In Berkeley it's possible
    to be white-haired and beautiful.

I avidly look at women with long white hair.
I walk fast, catch up with them, and look at their faces.
They're always beautiful.
They always smile back at me.
Always.

SPRING HARVEST

chapter three

What about dreams? What about them? They blur and leap; they hide, and they reveal. They feel like poems. Except without words. There's flight, there's music, but few words. My people in dreams rarely converse. Can I fly to poetry via dream? Find the words for the dream and have my poem? A dream will segue so naturally into morning sometimes, I move through the day sorting what's dream, what's real. Awake, the task would be to put visuals, feelings, ideas, beings into words.

Waking, my eyes project ribbon lines of green
computer letters everywhere I look.
I can almost read them ~
     rebuild the City ~ apple trees and yucca and palm ~

sirens ~ a blue house, a half-done house, a cemetery on
    the ridge ~

No, I am shaping/forcing sense. They're only letters of the
alphabet streaming past, and do not spell words. They fade, to
return another morning or night. (Eye doctors haven't heard
anybody else complaining about seeing letters of the alphabet.
"Seems harmless." "It could be your memory. You're remem-
bering reading and writing.")

Shadows of apple leaves on a white column.

> Rain in the morning
> Rain in morning in bed
> like cooking sounds
> the world set in motion
> while I stay in bed
> as if my mother alive again
>
> Another waking up:
> Waking up,
> I should smile
> at the new light in the corners
> but I want to put a bullet

through my throat.
No more consciousness.
No more.

Oh no, such unhappiness cannot be poetry. I refuse that one.

Inventing by dream
I have invented a bell. Hit
with wooden spoons and silver spoons
all the pots and lids and jars in the kitchen,
and decide which sound good to the ears.
Breathe and listen.
The wok lid is okay, not as deep as it looks.
The steel bowls without handles bong well,
each and every one bongs well.
Dream ceremony: Enemies come with potluck
    dishes.
They say their graces in this tradition and that
    tradition.
The atheist says something nice, kind, yet
    atheistic.

All eat. They like the food. They like one
    another.
They ring the bells. A bell is always near.

Spring rain—
    beads on the railings,
    mist in the hills.
Gladness in heart and home,
    relief after drought,
    high blooming clouds for two days.
A stork—a crane—but cranes flock—a stork
    stands on the roof across the street,
    lofts and lands on the next roof,
    and flies southwest.
I run after it, then run home and
    identify it. It's the great blue heron.
The great blue heron is possible in the city.

Thursday
Soft morning light on warm wood.
How could anything be wrong with me or anyone?

Small white clouds.
I can spoil anything and anybody with worry.
In nature on t.v., no sooner get to enjoying the life-cycle
    of whatever beast or bird,
but it's endangered, and all its kind dying out.
Extinction. The end.

Friday
After two days of heat that melted freeways,
I watch a movement of hazy lines -
    virgal rain?—march into a hill—smoke?—
straight from the ocean, thick gray source,
a cloud shooting low through the hills, and low on the street.
The cemetery on the hill fades,
    disappears, then suddenly, is clearly there.
Clouds are rushing in the sky.
A cloud is sitting on the ground.
I stand in it but cannot touch it or examine it.
At the moment, the state of my psyche corresponds
to the world I see. An awareness floats and blows
through and about things, comes and goes,

fades and clears. This attention is love,
and I can send it to people and animals,
situations and places. This attention is thought.
I curl and loop around and enwrap and permeate
every being and thing, and tie them to me and all to all.

Tax Day

Since beginning this poetry regime on the first day of
Spring, I notice a joy shimmering about the edges of things.
The balconies are leaking, the roof of my studio also leaking;
5 double true light windows have failed. An oil tank may be
buried in the backyard. That light, as long as I keep noticing it,
will not go out.

April 16th Sunday—

I saw a picture of a mass grave in Rwanda.
Like bones had been sorted with like.
All the skulls together, the heads right side up.

The same length arm bones in a pile,
the leg bones in another pile.
All is neat and orderly.
The people who did this stacking
show care for those who died.

I dreamed that it was El Día de los Muertos. Toy Day-Glo skeletons covered the fairgrounds.

Ching Ming was the 15th day after the Spring Solstice. I lost track, and did not go to my parents' graves. Good thing I have brothers and sisters who don't forget. They bring food, paper, whiskey, red flowers, roses, glads, geraniums, and incense and/or cigarettes.

MaMa has been dead 3 (?) years.
I'd heard a promise that in four
years, the mourning would change
from pain at loss to feeling her

presence in all the Earth ~
the trees, the hills, the air.
From the moment my father died
9 years ago, I see him in clouds,
and he is the Rabbit in the full moon.
My mother is not everywhere.
She seems to be in me.
Somehow, I continue her
whenever I am happy in the trees, the hills, the air.

I miss my baby boy.
I dreamed: My son drove back—he'd left early
to change his hair blond.
What has become of my dark-haired boy?
Oh, here he is, the baby in my arms.
I climb in the van and show him the baby he used to be.
Morphing boy to man, man to boy,
he rechanges, has thick dark hair.
Oh, this is a dream. "We're in a dream.
We can do anything. We can fly. Come on."
I hold baby and boy in left arm and by left hand,
and husband by the right hand.

They argue that we are real, not dream.
Real and heavy, we bound like kangaroos.
Bound bound bound.

One-year-old Baby Party

The newest baby girl can walk five steps.
Her second cousin, the penultimate baby, a boy,
    walks farther.
I bring raspberry shoots for everybody to grow
    in their yards.
Our parents liked gardening; now we like gardening.
Nowadays, the bakerman throws in for free a small
    round cake
for the birthday baby to moosh her hands and face into.
We don't teach her that funny American custom.
Baby's step-grandfather is a Korean War vet.
In the stairway, there's a picture of him with a rifle.
The baby loves light, and points to lamp, chandelier,
fishtank, and makes sounds to them.
She raises the dimmer switch—brighter, brighter.
She walks her five steps from one relative to another.

One of her great-uncles, my brother, says,
"The average child has two toys."
That can't be American children,
who have roomfuls of toys, shelves of dolls and
    teddy bears.
The 6 of us had played with one doll. "Our doll."
(She's over at George's house.)
I say, "Lucky."
My mother's, baby's great-grandma's voice comes
    out of me.
"Baby lucky."

I can find moments but not days for writing poems. Musicians—our son is a musician—have day jobs, yet sing and play. Poets write essays; poets teach.

Is the teaching in the way?
What I like about teaching:
Waves of good feelings pass between the students and me.
What hurts me teaching—
the shut-off person in the back row
who will have none of it.
She won't cross my path; I can't easily

take her aside, and advise her, Learn.

Wake up.

Let her go.

She'll just have to get information from books.

At the start of teaching and writing longbooks,

I would have gone out of my way,

looked up her file, phoned her, phoned her parents,

insisted that she see me after class, after school.

Now, I'm letting her go.

I went to hear the prize-winning poets from

   California colleges,

from two of my hometowns, Berkeley and Stockton.

50 poets, three of them my students, mostly women,

had minutes to read a poem or two. Hold your applause.

All the world's languages accented their English.

A Mexican American man read as "a Macedonian man":

"If it rains, take cover. There is poison in the clouds."

The women's lines ran like so:

"I love him bone and filth . . ."

"I could watch you all day the way you eat."

"I love his [something] ivy curling in like summer roses."

"My soul turns when I see you."
I, their elder, clapped loudly, alone, clapped
brava for my student from Persia.
You go, girl. You go, Poet.

I've discovered what stanza breaks are for. In the space,
breathe. Before and after the poem, breathe. I can pause, raise
my hand, and conduct your breathing.

Sunday April 30th. Open house to sell the old house.
The garden has been professionally and
    personally improved.
I spread new fertilizer and planted annuals.
I hired a housecleaning service,
and myself cleaned the house and windows again.
The to-be-sold house has been earthquake retrofitted,
lead abated, painted inside and out. The
    basement cemented.
No oil tank buried underground.
No oil tank connected to the rusty upthrusting pipe.
I am at order.
At our own house, I washed and put away the dishes,
vacuumed everything, washed my white sweater 10 times,

put the pots of jerusalem cherry together.
Now for a week of social activities.
People, don't you ruin my order.

~   ~   ~

           Social Activities (To Be Civil)
A lady party.
     Women coo. "So cute." "Oooh, how cute." "So nice."
     Tea, sushi, saké too. Pretty cakes and favors.
A wedding with bridesmaids in black cocktail décolletage
     at the communion rail. Mouths open for the host.
     Jesus' body lies on a pierced, studded tongue.
     They are down-to-earth in thick-soled shoes.
     Each face and hand shows stark and naked.
Houseguests from Hawai'i here,
then all of us houseguests at another friend's.
     Lie in the hammock together,
     pick strawberries, cook, eat,
     rollerblade against the wind
          and with the wind,
          chase the horses on the parallel bridle path,

play with Emma, who is two,
and Blaise, the dog, named after Blaise Cendrars.
At dusk, lock up the chickens (against raccoons
    and pumas).
The next day, stroll Main Street, Half Moon Bay,
    with the Pentecost Sunday parade of Big Queens,
Little Queens, and Side Maids,
visiting Queens of San Leandro, Hayward, Oakland,
    San Francisco.
You can go into the churches and be fed meat.
We bought rocks, a lamp, books, and sat at an
    outdoor café
and ate focaccia and ice cream.

~   ~   ~

May 4—Selling in a seller's market.
We sat like King and Queen
listening to bid after bid, higher and higher.
The realtors tell stories on behalf of the
    would-be buyers –
the adorable couple,

the darling, wonderful couple,
the unusual, artistic couple,
the inexperienced first-home couple,
the experienced couple, who want a city
    home-away-from-home,
the family whose little boy wants to live in the
    potting shed.
"Grandma can live in the garage."
They love the period stove, the cove ceiling,
the plate railings, the molding, the poppies,
the fig tree, the breakfast room with airy windows
that open to the tops of the lemon tree.
They love the kind people of Berkeley.
"Your home was made for grand occasions."
"We'll have two children."
"We work in San Francisco, and can commute
    from the curb."
All of them work in advertising and computers.
"We'll take good care of your home.
We know we'll be happy in it, as you were happy."
We didn't accept the highest offer but the one
the cleanest of contingencies.

Twice what we'd paid 8 years ago.
"Lucky," say my siblings and their spouses.
"Treat us to a sea cruise."
We go every day to the sold house,
water the new plants and window boxes of petunias,
check lights, locks, garage doors, wipe glass.
The house feels fragile. Please stay put.
Don't fall down. Escrow soonest.

May Day 2000   aerobics class

Terrific—the moment when we step sideways
then turn forward moving toward the mirror
and banking on the turn
altogether like a swarm or flock or herd wheeling ~
individual bodies, mine too, traveling in accord.

Cinco de Mayo ~ clouds like baleen, as if whales flying over

Tonight, a reunion of 20 of us from high school, the
class of '58.

Some of us first met as 4- or 5-year-olds, and some
    last seen on graduation day.
I look into a face, and suddenly recognize the little boy
    or little girl
or romantic teenager to whom I hadn't known
    what to say.
Nobody orders alcohol, so I don't either.
We hadn't been drinking as kids, and had good times.
We talk about our spouses and children
    and grandchildren,
our worries over them. Ruby Woo says, "I never worry.
If you can do something about it, do it.
And if there's nothing you can do about it, forget it."
The men take pictures of the women all in a group,
and the women take pictures of our boys, now men.
"Aren't they cute?" say the women. "Better-looking older."
"Better dressed." "Well seasoned." "And we
    passed them up."
Quite a few guys mention a first marriage and
    divorce. "She was a—"
"—a blonde bimbo!" the women chorus.

What happened to the rest of the 261 graduates
    in our class?
Only 20 out of 261 had the spontaneity, the curiosity,
    the success, the findability,
the drop-everything schedule to be at this impromptu
    reunion of Dragons,
helping one another turn 60 in this Dragon year.

May 12, 2000 Friday

Last night came dream-answers.
I am in bewitchment to change everything into words.
By day, writing, enwording . . . What's the urgency?
    The use? The good of it?
                        . . . only pleasure . . .

    Spring harvest of snow peas ~
They're taller than me.
I taste and eat as I pick along,
    choose the flat big ones and baby ones,

and leave the bulging pods for shelling or seed.
The purple and lavender blossoms
and the blue blossoms wave above me
and touch my neck.
I stand on the ledge of the box, reach for more,
and remember my mother and father growing
    snow peas every season.
When she could hardly see anymore, my mother
    showed me
by feel how to plant 3 seeds per mound.
Every day, enough for dinner, and for leaving
    at neighbors' doors.
The birds surround me and eat and sing. I am
    unequivocally happy.

~   ~   ~

Sebastopol—Now I am in the country. I'm leading war veterans in a tricky maneuver. At the same time, we'll live this day for itself and as rehearsal for next weekend. Friday night, read

stories and poems at the Unitarian Church in San Francisco.
Then all day Saturday at the Zen Center at Green Gulch Farm,
hold a writing retreat with the public.

Dreaming Awake

I have imposed a quiet. I have to impose it,
still myself, still the others.
Find the natural quiet.
Do I hear it yet? Is there such a thing?
The air is filled with bird song—
and airplanes and cars—motors—
insect motors, tractor motors.
Does an underlying, permeating stillness
contain the space-filling noises?
Time can. Idea can.
The red-tailed hawk is circling smaller and smaller.
Flashback—Earthquake! Bomb!
Radioactive light rays laser and scissor every place.
The brick road is buckling. Bricks entomb children.
I call for Earll—he's all right.

I have an excuse—Earthquake! Bomb!—
to cancel classes and miss appointments.
No, I need to get to school, to teach the children.
I walk over and through the rain of bricks ~
and wake up, and go again to school.

In the Meditation Hall at Green Gulch Farm, May 20, 2000

turning 60 in 5 months ~ June July
   August September October ~
I notice that the Buddhas have long ears.
Even the young Buddhas have long ears.
It was beautiful in Asia to be old and
   have long ears.
Heavy earrings and hearing stories, calls,
   cries pull ears long.
Are my ears too long? Keep them
   covered with my hair.

Through old woods, eucalyptus, pines, and bushes
of Cecil Brunner roses as high as a house,

I come upon a small hidden garden,
and am sitting on a bench in the sun.
Maybe I shouldn't be here. The garden
belongs to whoever lives in that little Japanese house.
He raked paths of gravel curving around young pines
and new-planted maples and large hewn or worn stones,
which he deliberately set beside the front door
and certain trees and a mossy mound. A bamboo
    fence winds
through the center of the garden, and a low wall
    surrounds it.
All is order. Exactly noon.
Sunny and shadowless. Weedless.
I would never build a garden like this one. My garden
has no fences. My house has glass doors.
If someone finds me and questions me, What are
    you doing here?
I have stolen into your garden,
and am taking a rest, and some privacy and time.

Non-poetic

worries

    that my students will boo the weird final exam.

    that the final will fall on the same day as the writing

        retreat.

    that none of the vets will want to read at the

        Unitarian Church.

    that too many vets want to read, and not enough time.

    that the little lost dog will have to stay with us.

    that the double true light windows have failed, and

        the glazier won't fix them,

        and won't pay for the ruined floors.

    that CalPERS will not sell us long-term care insurance.

    that nobody will come hear me lecture and the vets read.

    that too many or too few people will come to Green

        Gulch, and no prose muse will show up, let alone the

        poetry muse.

Getting money closing escrow on the house (where we lived
    after the fire),
  I have a desire to buy back the longbook.
  Return the advance, and not have to publish.
  And so The End.

    Idea!: Four-word poems!
    An old Chinese tradition.
    Easier, faster than haiku.
    To carve on rocks.
    To write on doorjambs.
    To write on thresholds.
    To tattoo on arms.
    Anybody can write one.
    Form takes no time.
    "Father Sky Mother Earth"
    "Raid kills bugs dead" —Lew Welch
    "Beyond mountains more mountains" —Lazy Old Man,
      my father
    "Across rivers more rivers" —Old Idle Man, my father
    Father gone Rabbit moon.

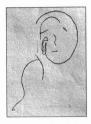

Giant anthuria Mother's Day
Sun beams me love.
Redwood tree one seed.
Strawberry Creek be free.
All rivers be free.

The oldest prayer is a four-word poem:

"May all beings be happy."

Well, that's sayable in four words in Chinese.

"All beings be happy."
"All beings be peaceful."
All beings be kind.
"All beings be free."

text.

That line about being kind, I made up. A very American four-word poem. Kindness takes going into action.

> They sing, they're happy.
> We eat our fortune.
> Time can. Idea can.
> Infinity ribbon circles all.

And there is such a thing as a two-word poem! And five- and seven-word poems. And the ultimate: the one-word poem! "Fook!" "Shou!" Oh, to say it all at once—one resounding word.

My father named me Ting Ting after the four-word poem: "Ting ting doak lup" ("Standing alone as a mountain peak"). Those sounds are pleasant to the Say Yup Chinese ear. Lone travelers—monks, ghosts, lovers, free and independent spirits, poets—meet at the pavilion under the lone pine upon the hill. Stop, listen, burn offerings in the ting.

May 29   Memorial Day
    Nhu, a Vietnamese American friend, has returned
        from Cuba,
    and advises me to go. My father lived in Cuba.

"You should go.
Everything you('ll) love is there.
And they will love you.
They love Las Chinitas.
But more than Chinitas—
they love Vietnamitas.
Listen to the songs.
They sing, 'La Chinita, La Chinita.'
I walk down the street, and they say, 'La Chinita.'
I say, 'No, no, yo soy Vietnamita.'
And they say, 'Ooooo, Vietnamita.'
Every little village has a street named after a
   Vietnamese freedom fighter.
Some *I* never heard of.
You're going to love Cuba."

June 1

I'm learning a new thing—tapdancing.
I'll learn meter, tapdancing.
I'll get rhythm, tapdancing,
my whole body gettin' rhythm, gettin' meter.

I am in time!
No worry about the future,
no rue for the past.
    I am in time!
    I am happy!
    time-steppin'
  double-time steppin'
  three-time steppin'
  four-time steppin'!
    waltz cloggin'
    shimshamin'
  stompin' and stampin'
    paddle rollin'
    heel diggin'
    toe hittin'
cramp rollin' cramp rollin'
    The Essence
    I am happy.
Every tapdancer is happy.
The bag lady dancing in slippers
is happy. No tragic tap.
  shuff-full, fal-lap, I-rish

ball change, ball change
shuf-full, ball change
maxi ford, anti-maxi ford,
Susie Q, Susie Q
The Earll
lunge ta-da hands ta-da hands
". . . the Candy Man can . . ."
". . . Santa Baby . . ."
". . . my heart belongs to Daddy . . ."
". . . the devil and the deep blue sea . . ."
Gonna tap my way to poetry.

Rollerblade with Bessie on Friday.
Saturday, John's 60th birthday party.
Easter Sunday at 11:00 A.M. the world meditating upon,
    praying for, thinking about Peace.
Sunday morning, Protection Ceremony for Vijaya and the
    twin girls in utero.
Sunday afternoon, read epithalamium at Maryanne and
    Brian's wedding.
Tuesday, Buddhists meeting to keep yet another sangha
    from schism.

Wednesday, farewell dinner with my students.

> Dominic from Viet Nam thought of it.
> "Bring real food. I can't believe frozen pizzas."
> I bring rice. Dominic's mother made spinach with
>   shrimp sauce.
> Jessica made piroshki.
> Lots of greens, salads, vegetables. Salmon. Wine.
> James brings a bottle of white wine.
> (Dominic ventured "liquor-free" for Mother's sake.)
> Shane, the ballplayer, orders a delivery of hot pizzas.
> They have memories of one who dropped out
>   of the course.
> "Remember? She and her boyfriend arranged to meet
>   on a hilltop
>   on a certain night in their dreams."
> "It's hard enough to find the right hilltop or right street
>   corner wide awake."
> They are from everywhere and going back, or on to
>   a new place.
> "Traveling the world—that is the story of
>   our generation."

"We don't feel the need for stability."

I return their portfolios while saying goodbye.

I am shooting babies into the wilderness.

"Let's meet again in your book."

Last night, a play in a series by playwrights who have been jailed, who have been executed.

I care about theater in warehouses and basements and livingrooms and lofts and storefronts and storebacks.

8 hours' rehearsal, and the play goes on. It gets heard.

Mother's heart and Sister's heart break as they identify and gather up the body of the young, tortured, dead hero.

Such torture never occurred to me: earphones plugged into his ears make sounds that break his mind, and kill him.

Every week, another play about the underdogs in a war for a cause that has gone on for centuries and continues to this day.

I wish I were at a cheesy/cheery musical.

But I return for the next act, the next play. What to make of it?

~   ~   ~

Sunday, Father's Day near Kapaʻau
Leina-a-kaʻuhane, place where souls leap off.
Kamehameha built the temple to Kū right
    here on Puʻukoholā.
Kū-kāʻili-moku, Kamehameha's image of war.
The last time I was on her Big Island,
Pele struck my head blind.
"Take that, Woman Warrior.
You call yourself Woman Warrior, do you?"
(I feel superstitious, breaking kapu saying those
    names aloud.)
I'm on the lookout, but this time do not sense her.
She knows that I'm unimportant.
The land feels mild today.
That breathing breathing breathing is the ocean
    in the east.
Sun and gentle rain all morning.
The sharma thrush sings long notes.
Choruses of small birds dee dee dee.
Choruses of doves diu diu diu (a dirty word
    in Chinese).

In the Poi Shack, the bathroom has glass walls.
Wild pigs and cattle watch us bathe.
Earll and I are the only people here.
You can safely leave the doors open.
I lock them from the inside before bed.
Alone, Earll and I panic.
How are we going to get back?
We should've flown into Kona, not Hilo.
What are we going to do?
You can't go over the Saddle Road in the rental car.
How to go back and forth quick, Hilo, Kona, Hilo?
All my fault, trying to meet our son's ship twice.
I begin the vacation (I never vacation)
making phone calls, changing times and places,
changing car, plane, hotel reservations,
canceling Kona, booking Honolulu,
talking and FAXing my agent re: longbook.

The banyan roots dangle from the top of the canopy
down to the singing, playing stream.
I think: Eden is not gone.

Earll and I are walking through Eden,
sometimes holding hands, sometimes
walking one behind the other, talking
and not talking. My most loving
person. Married 37 years.
Two animals we'd never seen before trot about
and nibble this and that. Not rabbits, not goats,
sheep, nor baby llama. Streaks of red,
sudden red flashes in the green,
are cardinals. Doves purr. That constant chirp—
finches. The white dart planes—mynahs
plunging, laughing squirt squat chicle chicle
greek greek greek greek!
Earll says, "Teach them the song from 'Birds.'"
Hoofprints of wild pigs. (At night—the snorts
     of wild pigs

eating macadamia nuts. Feral cats squalling.)
Fire ants act individually, no two rushing to
     the same place.
Clouds looping, scalloping, smiling,
Fronds arrowing into/out of trunks that circle
     like springs.
Black shaggy shadowy spheres of coconuts.
I see little yellow flowers seeing. Petals are
     their eyes.
Orange flower detaches from stem—orange
     butterfly.
Dark underbrush squiggles alive. The air alive.
          OCEAN   OCEAN   OCEAN
Time   My time
is moving at the rate of the wind in the trees. My time
moves back and forth, waving hello, waving goodbye.

     Earll is playing with a cow.
     The two bumps are Earll's knees,
     the curves the cow's horns,
     the loop a nostril, the gyres eyes,
     the white expanse cowhide,

the jet-black sparkles flies,
these lines the cow's legs,
and these Earll's legs.
Word or picture cannot show
the Reality of Cow.
She pushes her nose through the fence,
snorts, sprays snot—she drools cascades,
constantly looking at me with enormous eyes.
Why is she interested in us?
Big alive thing pushing through.

June 21, 2000   The Summer Solstice
Rained all night.
Yesterday was the last day of Spring.

Time's up. Whatever Spring poetry was to come has come.
Gary Snyder says that in a good year, he harvests 10 to 15
usable poems. That's only 2 or 3 per season. I think I can cull 2
or 3 writings—4 words at least—that I'm eager to read to peo-
ple. I held out my hands, and something came. I had a hap-
pening Spring.

June 26th—Joseph's birthday, Hilo

I can't quit this notebook before Joseph's Birthday.

> On his birthday eve, not knowing his parents
> are watching from our balcony, our son
> pedals his bicycle across the bridge,
> carrying his sweetheart standing on the rigs
> (rigs rigged to the hub of the back tires).
> She rides behind, holding on to his shoulders.
> They are very entertaining. They're entertainers.
> I love them.
> They talk and sing, sing and talk.
> "I heard a mockingbird with an infinite
>   repertoire.
> He and I stayed awake all night."
> "I heard a sharma thrush who
>   remembered long long riffs."
> "'When we're out together dancing face to face.'"
> "'Cheek to cheek.'"
> "I don't like 'cheeeks.'"

"'East of the sun, and west of the moon...'"
"I love those heartbreak songs."
"Aia la o Pele i Hawai'i ea—
E ala, E ala ea."
She chants Pele with a Hoboken accent.
Pele does not strike her down.
Pele loves her Haole child.
As Mother, I give advice:
Just one thing to do about life—
enjoy it. Enjoy it.

At the end of Spring
the ending of the longbook:

   Jik jik jik. Jik jik jik.
   Fa Mook Lan is weaving
   the shuttle through the loom
   when news of the draft comes.
   Each family must provide one man
   to be a soldier in the army.
   Sparing her dear father

the wretched life of a soldier,
she disguises herself as a man,
and goes in his stead to war.
With a horse, heavy armor, and
her hand-fitting sword,
she fights wars.
She is away long years,
and many battles, so long a time
that her father and mother grow old and die.
At the head of her army, giving chase,
and being chased,
she suffers wounds; blood drips red
from the openings of her armor.
Her army, chasing and
being chased, passes
her home village six times, back
and forth past her home,
but she cannot stop to place offerings
on the graves. At last, the invaders
flee the country, the war is done.
Fa Mook Lan leads her army to her home village,
and orders them to wait for her in the square.

Indoors, she takes off man's armor.
She bathes, dresses herself in pretty silks,
and reddens her cheeks and lips.
She upsweeps her long black hair,
and adorns it with flowers.
Presenting herself to the army, she says,
"I was the general who led you.
Now, go home." By her voice,
the men recognize their general—
a beautiful woman.
"You were our general?!" "A woman."
"Our general was a woman." "A beautiful woman."
"A woman led us through the war."
"A woman has led us home."
Fa Mook Lan disbands the army.
"Return home. Farewell."
Beholding—and becoming—Yin—the Feminine,
come home from war.
Jik jik jik. Jik jik jik.

I am ending the longbook with a poem. All that prose
added up to this one poem. If I hadn't put myself into a poetic

state, I wouldn't have thought to end this way. I went through a poetry door and came out of the war story.

So, I have had a season of poetry. And I'll have writing for the rest of my days . . . next, Summer Harvest . . . Autumn Harvest . . . Winter Harvest . . . then Spring Harvest again.